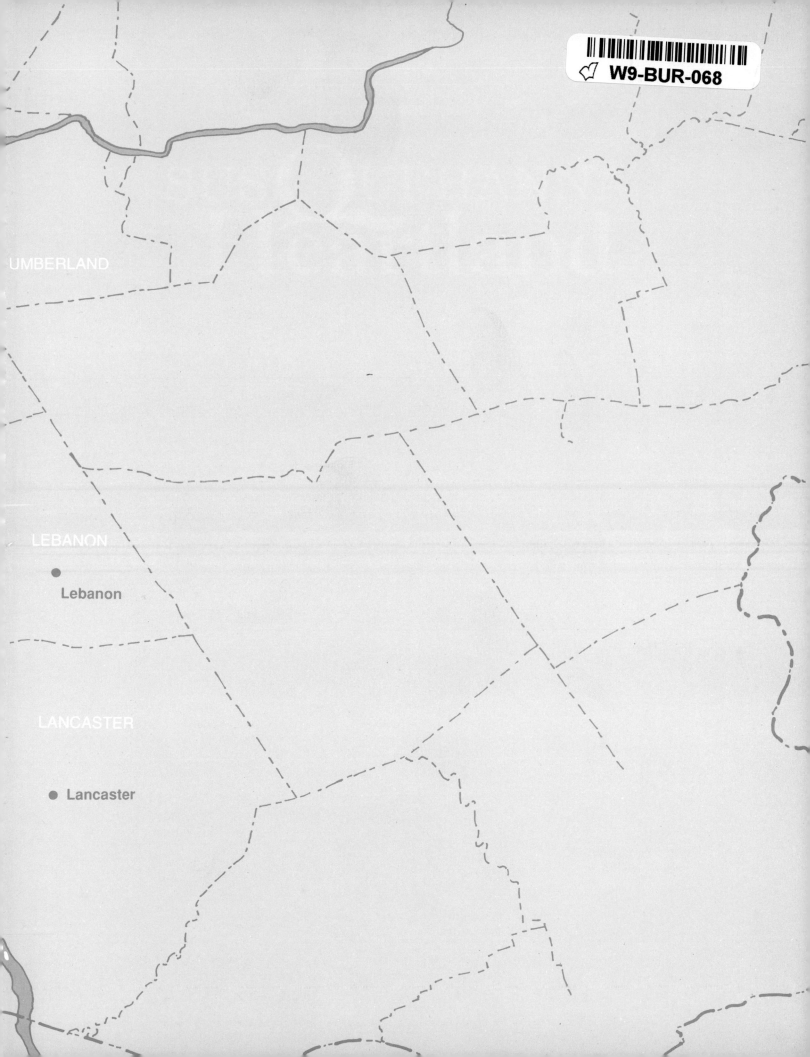

UMBERLAND

LEBANON

● Lebanon

LANCASTER

● Lancaster

Susquehanna Heartland
Text© 1992 by Ruth Hoover Seitz
Photographs© 1992 by Blair Seitz
ISBN 1-879441-78-0

Publisher's Cataloging in Publication
(prepared by Quality Books Inc.)

Seitz, Ruth H.
  Susquehanna heartland / Ruth Hoover Seitz, photography by Blair Seitz.
  p. cm. -- (Pennsylvania's cultural and natural heritage)
  ISBN 1-879441-78-0

  1. Susquehanna River--Description and travel. 2. Pennsylvania--
Description I. Title. II. Series. III. Seitz, Blair.

  F157.S8S4 1992   917.48
                                           QB191-2011

Published by

BOOKS

Seitz and Seitz, Inc.
1006 N. Second St., Suite 1-A
Harrisburg, PA 17102-3121

Design by Master Designs, Palmyra, PA
Styling by Nina Runk
Photo Research by Curt Sanders
Printed in Hong Kong

SUSQUEHANNA
Heartland

Ruth Hoover Seitz
Photography by Blair Seitz

Acknowledgements

DEDICATION

To those who contribute to the communities along the Susquehanna and to the health of the river itself without notice and without record. Your gift is with us and future generations.

The parameters of Susquehanna Heartland include the counties that border the main artery of the Susquehanna—Northumberland, Juniata, Snyder, Dauphin, Perry, Cumberland, York and Lancaster, as well as two others within the ridge and valley system, Lebanon and Adams. My thanks extend to all within the ten-county watershed who granted time to be interviewed and photographed. They live across the miles from the northernmost finger of Northumberland County to the Mason-Dixon line.

The efforts of folks in official capacities eased my own. Staff at the following organizations were most helpful in my initial search for contacts—Capital Region Chamber of Commerce, Gettysburg Travel Council, Hanover Area Chamber of Commerce, Juniata-Mifflin County Tourist Promotion Agency, Lebanon Valley Convention and Visitors Bureau, Northumberland County Tourist Promotion Agency, Pennsylvania Dutch Visitors Bureau, Perry County Tourist Bureau, Susquehanna Heritage Tourist Information Center, Susquehanna Valley Visitors Bureau and York Convention and Visitors Bureau. The historical societies within the counties did invaluable fact verification.

Various government bodies gave me access to data. I am grateful to people in the Pennsylvania Fish and Game Commissions, and the Department of Environmental Resources, especially the bureaus of Water Resource Management and State Parks. Thanks to the historians at the PA Historical and Museum Commission and to the curators at the State Museum of Pennsylvania for assistance. The city offices of York, Lancaster and Harrisburg were generous with information.

The staffs at the Chesapeake Bay Foundation, the Alliance for the Chesapeake Bay and the Susquehanna River Basin Commission were very supportive. I appreciated the observations of the naturalists at the recreation areas managed by Pennsylvania Power & Light Co. and Philadelphia Electric Co.

Most importantly, I am especially grateful to those who shared their experiences on the river and to friends who eagerly directed me to sites and sources for my own exploration.

All have helped to deepen my acquaintance with the river and its peoples.

—Ruth Hoover Seitz

Table of Contents

Pennsylvania's Largest River

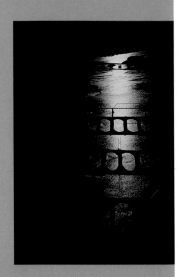

The view from Blue Hill chronicles the interplay of land, water and people in one little domain of the Susquehanna. Young trees on the bluff of Shikellamy State Park swish in the wind, catching the falling light from behind. A hundred feet below, the West Branch of the Susquehanna River joins its twin tributary from the north to create the biggest flowing river of the East Coast. Bridges span each of the three dark ribbons of fluid.

Yonder, the towns of Northumberland and Sunbury hug the shoreline, largely because the Europeans who pressed this far west in the 1700s found it as important to live along the river as the Native Americans who headquartered at Shamokin. A train rumbles below, and across river, a shifter lumbers past Northumberland's former Front Street Station. Bushy treetops on Packers Island mark the part of the state park where vacationers flock in the summer to fish, waterski and boat. A rubber fabridam creates 3,000-acre Lake Augusta which is deep enough for such recreation. It is deflated during off-season when rocks poke out of the water.

The river's shallowness is related to its age. The Susquehanna forged its course over the past 200 million years, wearing through layers of softer rock to the bedrock that cords its bottom. Old man river, one could say. To understand where the earth and river touched 40 million years ago when it wore away its present bed, one can stand beside the river and look a mile into the sky, suggests one geologist. Scouring over the centuries, it has been an active resource!

In other ways, the Susquehanna upholds its greatness. It pours drinking water for millions. It periodically submerges thousands of acres in water and untold numbers of people in grief. Its most recent flood, Hurricane Agnes in 1972, dumped over a million cubic feet per second into Maryland. The state's longest river, it snakes 444 miles from its rise in Cooperstown, New York to the Maryland border. Just below the Mason-Dixon line, it releases its watery wealth into the Chesapeake Bay at an average flow of 19 million gallons every minute. The river contributes half of the bay's fresh water.

The steep drop of the river's southern portion—a full 276 feet in elevation—created a natural environment for building hydroelectric dams. A century ago, the Susquehanna hurtled across rapids, cascading over falls, one with a drop of 125 feet, before it relaxed its energy in the Chesapeake, the world's largest estuary. Now four dams, in alphabetical order beginning from the south—Conowingo, Holtwood, Safe Harbor and York Haven—operate in a span of 45 river miles. Adding Muddy Run Pumping Station to the lot, they are equipped to produce 1,850 megawatts of hydroelectricity. This is more hydro power than all of New England's capacity. It is also more than ample for the Pennsylvania-New Jersey-Maryland grid that it supplies.

Two nuclear power plants, Three Mile Island and Peach Bottom, use river water for cooling processes.

The ferries of the 1700s disappeared with the building of bridges—except for the Millersburg Ferry, which has been plying a mile-wide stretch of the river in Dauphin County since 1817. Its two vessels, the Falcon and the Roaring Bull, are the only operating wooden sternwheel ferryboats in the United States. The curator for surface transportation at the Smithsonian Institution, Washington D.C., calls the Millersburg Ferry "a national treasure" because of the ingenuity of the ferrymen in devising a mode of transportation to get goods and people across such a wide, shallow waterway.

On many counts, the lower Susquehanna River holds sideshow status for the 1.5 million Pennsylvanians who live in its drainage basin. Although it is too shallow to be navigable, the river impacts living. The river stage is included with the local news. Residents picnic in parks overlooking its elegant bends. Folks enjoy its restful view from the office, hospital or living room window. Communities gather along its frontage for festivals and fireworks. Summer cottages with floating docks squat in flood-prone areas. The dams create "lakes" with recreational benefits; hundreds depend on their open water for skiing, wind surfing, sailing and hydroplaning. People can go fishing any old time.

The Susquehanna has always been a thoroughfare for freshwater species. Sports fishers pull in muskellunge, large-mouth striped bass, and a native river fish, the small mouth bass. Fall and later is prime time for walleye, a fish favoring cold water and the shelter of drop offs. Bass boats frequent the impoundments—Lake Shikellamy just below the joining of the West branch, Lake Aldred stretching eight miles between Safe Harbor and Holtwood Dams, Lake Clarke with over nine miles of backwater and Conowingo Lake just above the Maryland border.

But the American shad held supremacy over the length of this phenomenal river for centuries. Guided by a "radar thermometer" that signaled when the Susquehanna River had reached the preferred temp range of 58°-65° F, a school of shad traditionally swam north up the Chesapeake Bay from its wintering waters in the mid-Atlantic. A female shad first attempts the long trip from the ocean at four-to-six years of age, the male a year or so younger. Millions migrated upstream, 500 miles and more without eating, to spawn in the river each spring. There are accounts of farmers up north netting the weary shad, delighted to break the monotony of a cheerless winter diet. For them and the Native Americans before them, this fish with its tasty roe was spring bounty!

Shad runs gradually decreased. Dams and pollutants interfered with their life cycle. By the 1950s, people barely remembered the flavorful taste of shad baked until the bones became soft as flesh. As part of the cleanup of the Chesapeake Bay in the 1970s, naturalists lighted on technology that could restore the shad's spawning environment. Actually, that had been the reason for establishing the state's Fish Commission back in 1866. The project involves a hatchery along the Juniata, the Susquehanna's largest tributary, and the collection and trucking of migrating shad to release points north beyond the dams. A chemical mark on the earbone of each fish helps the government track returns.

It is natural for only 25 percent of the shad to swim downstream to the ocean after spawning. Each April, the shad run increases. Land transport could be dropped if the utilities that own the dams would install fish elevator systems. Since 1991, the first barrier, the 100-foot-high Conowingo Dam, has had an operating fish passage device. With many decades of effort, the Susquehanna is reestablishing a habitat for a shad fishery.

The overall health of the river has gradually improved from an all-time low in the '60s. Acid drainage from abandoned mines was checked. Wastewater treatment plants are now required to maintain water quality levels of inflowing creeks and streams. Fishing restrictions are strengthening other species besides shad. Proof of change came with the mid-80s return of the stinging black fly, which had avoided the river in its polluted state. Reducing silting and agricultural and recreational polluting are ongoing challenges to save not only a river, but a bay and its hundreds of thousands of living organisms. No wonder the following warning blazes culverts in many neighborhoods: "NO DUMPING. CHESAPEAKE BAY DRAINAGE."

(UPPER LEFT) Susque-hanna River from Chickies Rock Park, Lancaster Co. UPPER RIGHT) Sunset view of Lake Aldred formed by Susquehanna River from Pinnacle Overlook, Lancaster Co. (BELOW) The river reflects the lights of the Harrisburg skyline.

(UPPER LEFT) From Blue Hill, West Branch joins northern artery of Susque–hanna River with Northum–berland on left and trees of Packers Island on right.
(UPPER RIGHT) Holtwood Dam from overlook near Pequea, Lancaster Co.
(LOWER LEFT) Fishing boats near Selinsgrove.
(LOWER RIGHT) Newly-weds, Susquehanna River at Long Level.

(UPPER LEFT) Bob Neuhauser, Strasburg, explorer of river since boyhood. (UPPER RIGHT) Paddlewheel, Millersburg Ferry. (LOWER LEFT) Sunset river view from Walnut St. Bridge, Harrisburg. (LOWER RIGHT) From the Falcon, view of Roaring Bull heading west, the ferries at Millersburg.

(UPPER LEFT) Aerial view looking north from Wrightsville includes PA turnpike bridge. (CENTER) Fishing at sunset near Fort Hunter, Harrisburg. (UPPER RIGHT) Aerial, ice patterns in Susquehanna River, Dauphin. (LOWER LEFT) River during drought near a local rendition of the Statue of Liberty at Dauphin Narrows, Dauphin County. (LOWER RIGHT) Winter ice jam, Harrisburg.

(UPPER LEFT) Millersburg and view upriver shows its central plaza and rock dam below the ferry crossing. (UPPER RIGHT) Northwest view of bridges—road, rail and foot—crossing river from Harrisburg. (CENTER RIGHT) During usual idle fall interval, Three Mile Island Nuclear Power Station backgrounds river island farming. (LOWER RIGHT) Aerial view looking south along river, northern Dauphin Co.

History: Remnants of the Past

For 8,000 years hunters and gatherers gained nourishment from the land along the lower Susquehanna. Descendants of these early inhabitants cultivated and settled the heavily timbered watershed. At the beginning of the seventeenth century, the Susquehannocks planted corn, squash and tobacco at their riverine settlements—Conestoga, Washington Boro and near Wrightsville. With stone-chiseled arrows, they felled the animals that they needed for skins and meat. They crushed mussel shells gathered from the river to bind their clay to make pots. Fish such as shad, eels and bass, some several feet in length, seemed to reach for their bone hooks.

Occasionally, European adventurers appeared inland with a desire to trade. French explorer Etienne Brule traced the Susquehanna from headwaters to mouth in 1615-16. From 1630, guns became a coveted trade item. With their new firepower, several tribes of Native Americans overhunted and overtrapped, then pushed onward for new hunting turf. While in conflict with other tribes over land, they suffered from new diseases contracted from the rising number of Europeans. The Senecas overpowered the Susquehannocks, who scattered. After 12,000 years of development, the Native American population dwindled.

When the Quaker William Penn arrived to assume leadership of his proprietary land grant in 1682, he befriended the Native Americans and purchased land rights from their sachems. He assured these leaders that he and his followers "came not to injure others but to do good." He established a democratic frame of government aimed to do just that. For some years, a trusting friendship held between the Indians and Penn.

Today descendants of various tribes—Lakota, Seneca, Cherokee, Haliwa Saponi, Navajo, Choctaw and Passamaquoddy—live in the areas of Lancaster, Harrisburg and York. They share their culture at a yearly festival at Indian Steps Museum overlooking the Susquehanna at Airville. In the shade of mature trees, teepees and a totem pole, Native Americans drum and dance within a circle that is first blessed by a medicine person who turns to face each of the four directions.

With the dawn of the eighteenth century, the English, French Huguenots, Welsh, Scots-Irish and Germans poured into the new colony, named Pennsylvania for its founder and its deep green forests. The spillover from Philadelphia pushed toward the Susquehanna into an area of Chester County called Lancaster. One of the most striking English Quaker pioneers was Susanna Wright who lived in Wright's Ferry (Columbia) in a home built in 1738. Accepting the challenge of stabilizing a territory so far-flung when she arrived in 1726, Wright maintained correspondence with such forward thinkers in Philadelphia as Ben Franklin and James Logan, William Penn's secretary. Besides keeping abreast with intellectual trends, she studied botany, produced silk and developed rapport with the Indians.

A kindred frontier spirit was Joseph Priestley, a self-taught chemist who built a remarkable Georgian-style home overlooking the Susquehanna at Northumberland in 1796. After discovering oxygen in England, in Pennsylvania Priestley made the fizz that has been enjoyed ever since in sodas.

Some outlying settlements maintained forts to alert and supply settlers during the French and Indian Wars. Fort Augusta at Sunbury and Fort Hunter north of Harrisburg, both built along the River in 1756, protected farmers from frustrated Indians who were angered by the steady encroachment of whites beyond the Blue Mountains. In Carlisle, military expeditions were equipped and launched to cut through the wilderness and to defeat the raiding Indians. In a reconciling mood, Carlisle barracks held the only nonreservation school for Native Americans from 1879 to 1918. Jim Thorpe was among other athletes who trained there.

Some peasants who had been tenants in Europe squatted until they could purchase a parcel. Others answered Penn's advertisements to seek the religious freedom that his colony promised. Among the German religious groups were Amish, Mennonites, Moravians and communal pietists.

One of the finest examples of medieval Germanic architecture remaining in the United States is the Hans Herr House, the 1725 home of a Mennonite bishop. The Ephrata Cloister along the Cocalico Creek depicts the communal life of the pacifist followers of Conrad Beissel; in this austere setting, they drew intricate fraktur on their music manuscripts, printed German books and Bibles and nursed wounded Revolutionary War patriots.

In 1777, a congregation of Scots-Irish in western Lancaster County spontaneously left the service at Donegal Presbyterian Church when word arrived that the British were on the march towards Philadelphia. One of the worshippers, Colonel Alexander Lowery, asked volunteers to join hands around an oak tree to pledge support to form a new republic. The 400-hundred-year-old "Witness Tree" stood until it was felled by disease in 1991. These farm settlers shaped a self-sufficient environment with a do-or-die tenacity. At Donegal Plantation, a few miles from the Susquehanna, a sawmill, grist mill, ice pond, creamery and cider mill provided for this community's needs.

Most new immigrants farmed. By 1775, a third of the colony's settlers were Germans. The skills of their artisans produced the more accurate Pennsylvania rifle, the iron-plated stove, fine glassware and the Conestoga wagon, the tractor trailer of the eighteenth century.

When people saw hope for a water transport system in canals, they lured pick and shovel laborers from Ireland to build and maintain these watery networks. From 1825-1879 canals stretched from Sunbury to the Mason-Dixon line, a boundary with Maryland surveyed in the 1760s. The Union Canal, which connected the Susquehanna and Schuylkill Rivers, a project first recommended by Penn and pushed by Washington, operated from 1828 to 1884. Cutting a tunnel 243 yards long through a limestone hill near Lebanon completed the linking route. Various divisions of the Pennsylvania Canal, dug as a passageway from Philadelphia to Pittsburgh, handled thousands of boatloads of products up to 1901.

In the second half of the nineteenth century, railroads replaced the canals, steel production was in high gear, and coal was fueling homes and new industries. Between the Civil War and World War I, settlers and new waves of European immigrants plus Afro-Americans from the South ploughed their energies into manufacturing. Throughout the Victorian era, substantial building—ranging widely in ornateness—rose in cities and towns thriving with the help of railroads and electricity. The first electric lighting system graced Sunbury; the current went on July 4, 1883. Rural electrification arrived in the 1930s with many other public improvements such as state parks, dams, bridges and buildings such as Harrisburg's YMCA.

After auto production granted people more freedom than rail lines, interstates and the Pennsylvania Turnpike brought the ten counties along the main artery of the Susquehanna within easy reach of New York, Philadelphia, Baltimore and Washington D.C. Foodstuffs, home furnishings, industrial components and construction products left Susquehanna's heartland for urban markets. Except for the bridges spanning it, the river's role in this transport is now negligible. And the Susquehannocks leave no remnants save the inspiration that their namesake, the Susquehanna, still gives the 1.5 million Pennsylvanians who live south of the juncture of its West Branch.

(L.H. PAGE) Native American Tony Hedgepeth of York assembles regalia at Indian Steps Museum with river in background. (UPPER RIGHT) Conestoga wagon, State Museum of PA, Harrisburg. (CENTER RIGHT) Col. John Connors, Confederate officer, at Civil War battle re-enactment. (LOWER RIGHT) Blacksmith Bob Hanson at work colonial-style at Mill Bridge Village, Lancaster.

(UPPER LEFT) Burning glass used by Joseph Priestley, discoverer of oxygen, at Northumberland laboratory. (UPPER CENTER) Linden Hall, oldest girls' school residence, founded 1746, Lititz. (UPPER RIGHT) Foyer, Cameron Estate Inn near Donegal Presbyterian Church, home of Simon Cameron, Pres. A. Lincoln's Sec. of War. (LOWER LEFT) Hans Herr House, oldest home in Lancaster Co., built 1719. (LOWER RIGHT) Restored Railroad House built in 1820 during Marietta's canal and railroad era.

(UPPER LEFT) Gothic
Revival-style window of
Cornwall Furnace, only fully
intact 19c charcoal blast
furnace in U.S., Lebanon
County. (UPPER CENTER)
Children's playroom with
view of Rockville Bridge over
Susquehanna, Fort Hunter
Mansion, Harrisburg. (R. H.
PAGE) Exterior, Wright's
Ferry Mansion, Columbia
(LOWER LEFT) and dining
room, with fine 1700-1750
Philadelphia furnishings.

(UPPER LEFT) Food preparation was simple, Ephrata Cloister. (UPPER CENTER) Docents in white robes of Seventh Day Baptists at mid-18c Ephrata Cloister, Ephrata. (UPPER RIGHT) Donegal Plantation, a self-sufficient farm settled by Scots-Irish. (LOWER LEFT) Steelton, the river town making the first Bessemer steel, Dauphin Co. (LOWER RIGHT) Mennonites tracing their church history, Cumberland County.

(L.H. PAGE) Market Square. (UPPER RIGHT) Adults-Sharon Stevenson and Stephanie Mellott and children with catenary arch, Museum of Scientific Discovery. (CENTER RIGHT) Vonnece Mansfield jumping rope, uptown Graham St. (LOWER RIGHT) Coccia family picnicking, Italian Lake, Division and 3rd Sts.

31

(PREVIOUS PAGES) Rail bridge and skyline from Interstate 83 bridge. (UPPER LEFT) Multi-generation family singing as The Scott White Evangelistic Crusade. (UPPER RIGHT) Guitarist Matthew Dodd at annual Harrisburg Hiroshima-Nagasaki observance of "Candles on the Water." (LOWER LEFT) Enclosed atrium at Strawberry Square, formerly an alley. (LOWER CENTER) Mural by Neigh–borhood Center youth depicting area Underground Railroad events, 6th and McClay Sts. (LOWER RIGHT) Corner deli, artwork, Cameron & Market Sts.

(BELOW) Northwest view of Capitol Complex and State Museum of Pennsylvania (circular bldg.) (TOP, LEFT TO RIGHT) 1. View of Harrisburg and Blue Mountain, facing northeast. 2. Conrail Railroad Bridge in early morn. 3. Rockville Bridge, facing northwest.

(UPPER LEFT) A N. 2nd St. house, annual Candlelight House Tour. (UPPER RIGHT) Carriage ride along 3rd St. in front of PA's Capitol. (LOWER LEFT) Art show in restored mansion at Reservoir Park. (LOWER CENTER) Folk art clock made in Halifax by Wm. Gray as a wedding gift for his wife Catherine, John Harris Mansion, home of Dauphin County Historical Society. (LOWER RIGHT) Wm. McClay Mansion, 401 N. Front St.

WILLIAM MACLAY

In the stone house opposite lived William Maclay, who as a member of the first U.S. Senate, wrote a famous journal of its debates. A critic of Washington and Hamilton. Pioneer leader of Jeffersonian Democracy.

(PREVIOUS PAGE) Victorian decor, Fulton Opera House, 12 N. Prince St. (UPPER LEFT) Robert Fulton Birthplace, south of Lancaster on Rt. 222. (R.H. PAGE) Apse of St. James Episcopal Church, erected 1820, 119 N. Duke St. (LOWER LEFT) Rooftop facades, N. Queen St.

(UPPER FAR LEFT)
Dining room, home of
portrait artist Jacob Eichholtz
before his death in 1842.
(UPPER CENTER)
Steinman Park, one-half
block from Penn Square on
W. King St. (UPPER
RIGHT) Watt & Shand
Department Store, S.E.
corner of Penn Square.
(LOWER LEFT) Jacob
Eichholtz home, 46 S. Lime
St. (LOWER RIGHT) View
from tower of Holy Trinity
Lutheran Church showing
courthouse with clock tower,
Duke St., and white steeple
of 1877 First Presbyterian
Church, E. Orange St.
(EXTREME RIGHT)
Recent immigrants studying
English.

(UPPER LEFT TO RIGHT) 1. Lancaster's Central Market, built 1889. 2. Library, Wheatland, home of Pres. James Buchanan. 3. A multiple exposure made in black light room, North Museum, Franklin & Marshall College. 4. Astronomer Ralph Battaline in planetarium, North Museum, College and Buchanan Aves. (LOWER LEFT) Central Market stalls. (LOWER RIGHT) Lancaster's Penn Square with 1874 Soldiers and Sailors Monument to Civil War dead in center.

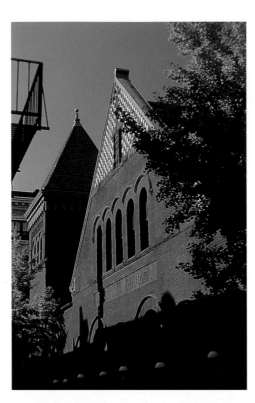

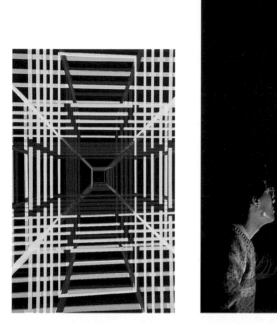

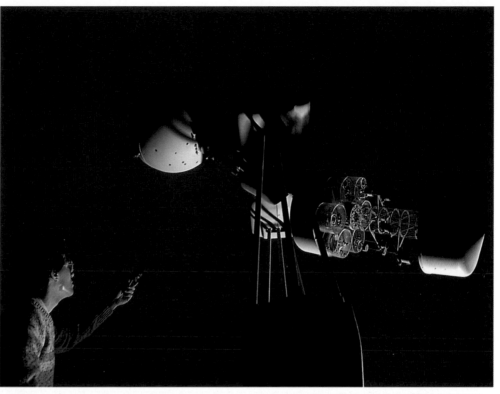

5

York: The Nation's First Capital

More than 250 years old, the city of York wears its past well. Several structures with an indelibly colonial connection stand alongside ornate Victorian and squarish modern buildings. Public property that serves up food, fun and fire protection—the Central Market, the York Fairgrounds and the Rex and Laurel Fire Station respectively—are strong favorites of Yorkers. Local loyalty runs solid. Spectators at the area's finest Halloween parade stake out a view three hours in advance. The third generation of the same families heap York fruits and baked goods at market stalls. And, from the Strand-Capitol, plays and classic films entertain in the restored vaudeville hall and 1920s movie palace.

York's location put it on the map, so to speak. The town was laid out in a checkerboard pattern in 1741 because settler Baltzer Spangler favored a town where the Monacacy Indian trail crossed the Codorus Creek. Thirty some years later when the British occupied Philadelphia during the colonies' fight for independence, the members of the Continental Congress fled to York so that the Susquehanna River would be a deterrent to enemy advance. In their sessions in the colonial courthouse, they wrestled with governing thirteen separate colonies as they struggled to stay warm by the heat of an iron-plate stove. On November 15, 1777, they adopted the Articles of Confederation, thus forming the United States of America. And so, York became the first legal capital of the nation.

The delegates referred to this rustic town as "little York" to distinguish it from Yorktowne in Virginia. Perhaps one of the "publick houses" they frequented was The Golden Plough Tavern with its Germanic half-timber construction and wooden chimney. Thanks to The Historical Society of York, the 1741 tavern and adjoining stone Gates House are furnished in the period and welcome visitors.

York's streets around Continental Square are lined with superb architecture such as the 1840 townhouse at 152 E. Market Street expanded in 1875, which was the home of artist Horace Bonham. The Billmeyer House is an ornate 1866 Italianate villa that features ceiling frescoes. The 1911 Fluhrer Building with its terra cotta facade reflects a later Italianate design. The Art Deco style GTE Building built in 1931 has relief panels of telephone linemen. Beaver, Duke and Philadelphia Streets boast many restored Victorian homes. Pfaltzgraff, the only American manufacturer of bone china, uses several for offices while preserving their residential appeal.

From his townhouse at 123 E. Philadelphia St., black businessman William Goodridge conducted many slaves to safety, hiding some in a straw-covered trench in back of his home. With much support from black residents, the Underground Railroad traffic was especially heavy in York between 1820 and 1850.

Descendants of the German and Scots-Irish craftsmen who settled in York excelled at manufacturing. Yorkers became makers of chains and cables, earth movers, weight-lifting equipment, air conditioners, motorcycles and many other metal products. While these factories beyond the city borders produce, downtown merchants and professionals perform services amidst some tokens of the past.

Passers-by can't resist peanuts roasting in front of Mike's Nut Shop, a 90-year-old endeavor along Market Street. Noon concerts in Cherry Lane Park draw downtown employees. Inside the warm-toned brick market, with its Romanesque arches and turrets, there are lunch choices-spicy sausages, crunchy apples and hand-dipped potato chips, all fresh. They are as delicious today as they were at the turn of the last century.

(PREVIOUS PAGE) Await–ing Halloween Parade, Market St. (UPPER LEFT TO RIGHT) 1. Cherry Lane street sign. 2. Lunchtime concert in Cherry Lane Park off Market St. 3. Joann Kopp cleaning ceramics after firing at Pfaltzgraff, the oldest continually-operating pottery manufacturer in the U.S., started in early 1800s in York County. 4. Award on display at Bob Hoffman Weightlifting and Softball Hall of Fame beside firm, York Barbell. (LOWER LEFT) Restored ceiling, The Strand Theatre, 50 N. George St. (LOWER RIGHT) Sheep judging, York Fair at 120-acre Fair-grounds, 334 Carlisle Ave.

(PREVIOUS PAGES) York Suburban Marching Knights, annual Halloween parade, W. Market St. (UPPER LEFT) Parlour, Bonham Hse.,152 E. Market St. (UPPER CENTER) Shopping, Central Market, 34 W. Philadelphia St. (UPPER RIGHT) York County Colonial Courthouse, site of Continental Congress Sept 1777 to June 1778, rebuilt 1976, 205 W. Market St. (LOWER LEFT) Victorian-style Rex and Laurel Fire Station,15 S. Duke St. (LOWER CENTER) Fluhrer Bldg with facade of glazed terra cotta built 1911, 17 W. Market St. (LOWER RIGHT) Barnett Bobb Hse., early 19c Germanic log home, 157 W. Market St.

6

Town Life Within the Watershed

Clocks, squares and plazas represent town centers as meeting and gathering places. Earlier in time when a personal timepiece was a luxury, town clocks aided shoppers in keeping track of train and trolley schedules. Today, clocks in Columbia, Mechanicsburg, Selinsgrove and other communities are landmarks.

Millersburg in Dauphin County spreads out as its founder, Daniel Miller planned—with a public park along the riverfront, sites for churches and a plaza in the square. The locals see each other at church, at school events, at the grange and around the gazebo during festivals. They do business in the town center. With the jewelry, shoe and hardware stores stands Leppert's 5&10, with its old-fashioned counter where customers select candy from glass jars.

Three river boroughs, Marietta, Columbia and Wrightsville polish images that include an industrial past. In the 1800s, Marietta thrived on lumber and commerce and later iron production. The 1790 River Inn and the Railroad House, both in the borough's National Historic District, serve guests now as they did in the past. What the 2,700 residents enjoy year-round is the character of the streets, unspoiled by traffic lights, and the friendly safety of a place where they can leave the back door unlocked for the plumber.

Downriver, beyond a majestic curve crowned by the scenic Chickies Rock rises Columbia, a borough of more than 10,000 inhabitants. Since the 1720s, the site was an important river crossing and a hub for canal, railroad and turnpike traffic and support industries. Since 1812, Columbia has been linked to Wrightsville by bridge. A mile-long bridge, built in the 1930s joins the two former ferry crossings.

Shrewsbury is a York County village that can be found on 18th century maps of Penn's colony; it was a stopover along the Susquehanna Trail on the way north from Maryland. A crossroads with one traffic light, the borough has remained residential since a German farmer named Baltzerfaust laid out the town. Free of store signs, its Main Street blooms with neatly painted Victorian-style homes, smaller log homes covered with siding and among the churches, one that plays chimes at dusk.

County fairs, which began in colonial times to unify the rural community, still bring people together. In Hanover, a town boosted economically by shoe and snack production, there is a parade and performances during "Dutch Days." On market day, an organ grinder entertains shoppers.

Eighteen miles from the Susquehanna, Carlisle reigns in Cumberland County as both a college and a military town. Dickinson College, founded in 1783 by Dr. Benjamin Rush, maintains a strong liberal arts tradition. Among its stone buildings is Old West, a striking 1804 post-colonial structure that was designed by Benjamin H. Latrobe, the architect of the Capitol in Washington D.C. The history of the Carlisle Barracks with its many training uses harks back to the arrival of a British battalion in 1757. Today it is home to the United States Army War College and The Military History Research Collection.

A town's shops, training centers, public buildings, parks and homes reflect the interests and attitudes of its residents. In many towns within the watershed, respect for the past is expressed through preservation and conservation. Town clocks, tolling bells and the noontime whistle signal the passage of time and the opportunity to restore and thus maintain some of the past within America's convenience store mindset.

(UPPER LEFT) Lebanon County Fair at fairgrounds. (UPPER RIGHT) Church crafts for sale, Littlestown Arts and Crafts Show, Littlestown. (LOWER LEFT) Beauty pageant, Shippensburg Fair, Shippensburg. (LOWER RIGHT) Dickinson College, a campus in center of Carlisle, pop. 17,500.

(PREVIOUS PAGES) Signs of restoration, W. Main St., Mechanicsburg. (CENTER LEFT) Lincoln Square, downtown Gettysburg. (UPPER RIGHT) Clogging during Historic Marietta Days, W. Market St., Marietta. (LOWER RIGHT) Gettysburg Brassworks in parade during Hanover Dutch Festival, Hanover.

7

Travel Attractions Within the Heartland

Like a magnet, the lush farm country and the plain-clothed Amish who till it attract visitors to Lancaster County from as far away as Japan. Even Philadelphia, the center of America's independence, draws fewer than the five million who annually head for Pennsylvania Dutch country. Cars with out-of-state license plates crawl along scenic backroads, stopping at well-kept farms selling produce, baked goods and hand-crafted products. Amish cottage industries serve their own as well as the visitors who "discovered" this Anabaptist Sect since the 1985 release of the movie, "Witness."

Some take a buggy ride and eat sweets and sours served Amish-style at a long table. Others gain an authentic interpretation of Amish faith and practices by hiring the services of a guide from the Mennonite Information Center and visiting The People's Place in the village of Intercourse. Many admire with puzzlement these real people living their own truth. Most leave with a yearning for simpler schedules and time with the land.

In Strasburg, The Railroad Museum of Pennsylvania houses restored locomotives and and exhibits of train memorabilia. On nearby tracks of the Strasburg Railroad, America's oldest short-line railroad, a steam locomotive chugs passengers across Lancaster's rich farmland.

Just 30 miles away in a place now named for him, Milton S. Hershey plowed a cornfield to build a factory that would use fresh milk to make a 5¢ chocolate bar. From 1904 the number of employees rose with production. Mr. Hershey responded to both by investing in attractions that still draw visitors to this "real home town" in Dauphin County.

Thousands flock to Hersheypark™, a theme park with more than 50 rides, including a magnificent hand-carved Carousel built in 1919 when this park offered "picnic and pleasure grounds" for employees. The bobcat and other North American animals at nearby ZooAmerica™ pay no mind to the screams descending from the roller coasters.

For decades, visitors toured the chocolate factory itself to see bars and kisses transformed from conched chocolate. Now they learn the story of chocolate-making at Hershey during an automated high-tech ride through Chocolate World. It is still worth a drive down Chocolate Avenue underneath the streetlights shaped like kisses to inhale the sweet aroma of cocoa beans roasting inside the plant.

Throughout the town stand well-constructed facilities "offering a variety of pleasant ways to spend one's time," as Hershey himself planned. Seventy-two holes of golf challenge both the novice and the accomplished.

At the grand Hotel Hershey, unrivaled chocolate desserts are served in the circular dining room free of columns so, according to Hershey, "persons who don't tip well cannot be put in a corner or behind a pillar."

Providing for the less fortunate guided Mr. Hershey's philanthropy. In 1909, he and his wife, Kitty, founded Milton Hershey School for orphan boys. Over the years, more than 7,000 boys and girls have graduated, many filling leadership positions in Hershey and around the world. Among its superb training facilities is Founders Hall, an artistic tribute to the Hersheys.

The grounds around Founders Hall provide a scenic backdrop for many a classic car. Each fall, thousands of car buffs motor into Hershey for the largest antique car show in the world. The 50,000-member Antique Automobile Club of America is headquartered here.

Southwest in Adams County, 1.5 million tourists a year visit Gettysburg National Military Park, the site of one of the most decisive battles in American history. For three stifling summer days, July 1-3, 1863, 70,000 Confederates waged combat with 92,000 Union troops. On occasion, the number of visitors to this Civil War battlefield tops the number that fought here.

By car, bicycle, horse or foot, visitors follow the movements of the two armies across rolling terrain that looks very much like it did before the battle. Near the High Water Mark of the Confederacy stands a memorial inscribed with the names of the nearly 35,000 Pennsylvanians who fought here. The Electric Map and Cyclorama presentations trace the battle. Pausing near breastworks or the rocks at Devil's Den brings back a sense of the battle scene-a noisy, smoke-filled atmosphere. It is redeeming to visit the spot in the National Cemetery where President Abraham Lincoln delivered his Gettysburg Address to dedicate this burial ground later that year. Acclaimed world-wide as a literary masterpiece, his two-minute speech is the only one honored by a monument.

The home of another president, Dwight David Eisenhower, invites tourists to Gettysburg. They stroll through the house and grounds where he and Mamie entertained dignitaries. The decor depicts the homey practicality of the 1950s.

It is at the Capitol building in nearby Harrisburg that people exclaim over ornateness. At its dedication in 1906, President Teddy Roosevelt declared, "It's the handsomest building I've ever seen." Italian Renaissance in style, the Vermont marble structure has more symbolic art and intricate sculpture than one can absorb during one of the free tours offered seven days a week.

A golden female figure titled "Commonwealth" tops the 52-million pound dome. The climb up the Capitol steps is long enough for visitors to get a good view of George G. Barnard's marble statuary guarding the bronze doors that each weigh a ton.

Inside, most striking is the Rotunda with its grand staircase sweeping up to the legislative chambers. Goldleaf rosettes, columns, medallions and eagles symmetrically garnish the dome and its cornice. Four recessed murals by Pennsylvanian Edwin Austin Abbey portray spirits directing goodness within the State. The third lunette shows The Spirit of Religious Liberty guiding ships of early settlers across the open sea to the New World.

The chamber of the House of Representatives is a splendid setting for the gathering of the oldest continuous democratically elected body in America. It was founded in 1682 by William Penn. Among the chamber's accouterments are mahogany paneling, stained glass, French marble, detailed murals and four-ton bronze chandeliers. Alas, there is no female among the famed Pennsylvanians in Abbey's 35-foot square "Apotheosis." On the ceiling mural, however, 24 maidens represent the passage of time.

With the 1987 construction of the East Wing, which includes offices, a public cafeteria and three levels of underground parking, the Capitol Complex was completed. It is refreshing to watch changes in the flow of water from 123 nozzles and three triads on the computerized fountain along Commonwealth Avenue.

The State Museum of Pennsylvania to the north of the Capitol merits repeat visits. Four floors of exhibits highlight Native Americans, wildlife, minerals, agriculture, decorative arts, tools and machinery—all related to Pennsylvania.

A tour of the riverside Governor's Mansion on 3.5 acres at McClay and Front Streets reveals period antiques and replicas as well as rotating art exhibitions.

The Susquehanna watershed figured heavily in the country's history. People visit these counties in the heartland to recapture their heritage. The scenic beauty of the river, mountains and farmed valleys heightens each experience.

(PREVIOUS PAGES) 1941
Packard, Hershey Antique
Auto Show, Hershey.
(UPPER LEFT) Pretzel-
making by Holly Tshudy,
Sturgis Pretzel House, Lititz.
(UPPER CENTER) Open–
ing of Little League World
Series, Williamsport, a town
along West Branch. (UPPER
RIGHT) Amish girl reads in
back of buggy, Lancaster Co.
(LOWER LEFT) Hot air
ballooning, Hershey.
(LOWER RIGHT) Amish
bring in hay near Smoke-
town, Lancaster Co.

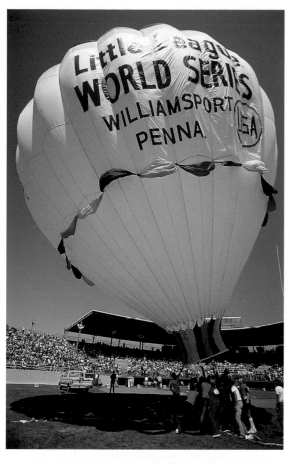

(PREVIOUS PAGES) Amish children from six families load wheat shocks for threshing, Lancaster Co. (UPPER LEFT) Living room, home of Pres. and Mrs. Dwight D. Eisenhower, Gettysburg. (LEFT CENTER) Governor's reception room, Capitol, Harrisburg. (LOWER LEFT) Baling during July wheat harvest, Amish farm, Lancaster Co. (R.H. PAGE) Dome, Capitol rotunda, Harrisburg.

(PREVIOUS PAGES) House of Representatives chamber, Capitol building, Harrisburg. (UPPER LEFT) Exterior, PA Capitol dome, Harrisburg. (UPPER RIGHT) Cannon used against Pickett's Charge, Gettysburg National Military Park, Gettysburg. (LOWER LEFT) Fountain, Capitol Plaza, Greater Harrisburg Arts Festival, Memorial Day weekend. (LOWER RIGHT) Memorial to 8th PA Cavalry near rail fence, Civil War battlefield, Gettysburg.

8

The Arts, Fine and Practical

The arts are fertile, thriving in both the cities and countryside on either side of the Susquehanna. Besides individual working artists, established groups teach and perform plays, dance and music from folk to jazz.

With encouragement from private patrons and business, Harrisburg is undergoing a renaissance. "Artists find the area nurturing, the land and river inspiring," says Carrie Wissler-Thomas who paints in oils. The thriving Art Association of Harrisburg and the crisp, non-profit Doshi have benefited from the input of teacher Charles "Li" Hidley and abstract surrealist Larry von Barann respectively. Wanda Macomber expresses her love of the area through her precisionist architecture. Two imports, Kathleen Piunti and Barbara Buer have developed their photo-realism here.

In Lancaster, David Brumbach, Lynn Yancha and Richard Ressel interpret their environments in watercolor. Carol Galligan uses an eclectic range of media for her abstracts. Some exhibit at the non-profit Community Gallery downtown. Several dozen artists work in studio/galleries at The Artworks, a former shoe factory in Ephrata.

Many working artists in York County transferred from an urban environment. All sought creative breathing room whether it was actual physical space or the emotional sustenance that they perceived to be too diluted in the city. It is not surprising to find artists in the hinterlands of the lower Susquehanna, e.g., the Fensters at The Stone Mill, Rob and Lucy Wood at Spoutwood Farm and David Kline at Family Heirloom Weavers.

Each artist's production is part of a self-styled package that also markets and sells what is created. Gallery visitors can watch Bill Lynch throw pots in a converted Snyder County gristmill. Dorothy Masom of Selinsgrove makes paintings from encaustics, dry pigment mixed with hot wax. She lectures on this ancient medium, which holds its brilliance through time and pollution.

Nature often inspires art. Recording observations in dozens of notebooks while hiking and hunting, Ned Smith, a Millersburg wildlife illustrator, drew animals and birds in their habitat. At his death in 1985, his work was in collections at the Carnegie Institute of Art and the Museum of Natural History.

Believing in the inspiration of nature, Ken and Sally Hassinger hold art workshops at their 175-acre property called The Water Co. Farm near McClure in Snyder County.

Arts and crafts shows and festivals enable people who create to showcase and sell their work. Held at Pennsylvania's Chautauqua, the juried Mt. Gretna Outdoor Art Show is one of the most discriminating. Some such as the Riverwalk Arts Festival in York, Little Buffalo Festival of the Arts in Perry County and Harrisburg's Memorial Day weekend bash are also venues for music performances. Members of the Pennsylvania Guild of Craftsmen show their work regularly.

Collectors follow woodcarvers who hold their own shows. Their skills range from carving working decoys, a specialty of Clair Koons, York, to sculpting wildfowl art pieces, the focus of York's Ken Thomas and Stan Pearson of Camp Hill. The carvings of Gettysburg's Iber Courson, Lancaster's Jim Hazley and York's Dale McCoy perform well in mid-Atlantic competitions. The teaching skills of carvers such as Doug Gable and Joe Kline have strengthened area carving clubs.

The pastoral surroundings of the river and the hills that it bisects create a setting that frees the imagination. The milieu of the Susquehanna prompts artistic expression.

(UPPER LEFT) Creations at Stone Mill—pottery by Inez Fenster, floral design by Carol Novak and table by Jerry Fenster, Brodbecks, York Co. (UPPER RIGHT) Doshi Center for Contemporary Art, Transportation Center, Harrisburg. (LOWER LEFT) One of the galleries of The Art Association of Harrisburg, 21 N. Front St., Harrisburg. (LOWER CENTER) Dave Brumbach (1948-1992) with his art at Demuth Foundation Gallery, Lancaster. (LOWER RIGHT) Wildlife paintings of the late Ned Smith, Millersburg.

(UPPER LEFT) Listening to the historic carousel band organ of Mt. Gretna during the village's annual outdoor art show, porch of long-time resident and historian, Jack Bitner. (UPPER CENTER) Harrisburg-based Old World Folk Band. (UPPER RIGHT) Bruce Johnson and his art, The Chimneys, Hershey. (LOWER LEFT) Artwork on display, Kipona Festival, Harrisburg's Riverfront Park. (LOWER RIGHT) Central PA Jazz Festival, an annual event in Capital Region.

(UPPER LEFT) A scene from Ingmar Bergman's NORA, A DOLL'S HOUSE by Henrik Ibsen presented by Open Stage of Harrisburg, a regional theater. (LOWER LEFT) Detail, beaded belt, dance instructor, Queen Holmes. (LOWER RIGHT) WO'SE Dance Theatre, an Afro-American dance experience, Harrisburg.

9

The Ways of the Countryside

Farming. Farmland. Sacred words, especially in the watershed of the Susquehanna River. The formation of the soil of area farmland began 300 million years ago. The compressing, buckling, and eroding of the earth that formed coal created a series of valleys and ridges—our Appalachian topography. Over thousands of years the limestone and shale areas wore down more quickly, becoming valleys between ridges of harder sandstone and quartzite. The Cumberland and Lebanon Valleys west and east of the Susquehanna are a portion of The Great Valley that runs close to a thousand miles from New York to Tennessee.

Any lookout over the Susquehanna's watershed unfurls a patchwork of farm country. Between angles of any degree, crops form fields of wavy alfalfa, stalky corn and dense grain. Farmers harvest bumper crops from those fields because the limestone content is naturally high. Creeks meander through meadows dotted with Holsteins. Houses pop up along ribbons of road or streams. The dwellings may be stone or brick put up in an era when it was crucial to live near flowing water.

Today's streams in these rich agricultural counties carry more than H_2O. Too often they bear too much of a good thing. Excess nutrients from fertilizers and manure run off the fields into surface water and seep through the earth into groundwater. Creeks and streams cannot dispense with what the crops cannot use. When levels of yield-boosting nitrogen, for example, soar beyond the useful point, they become polluting nitrates. Throughout the counties of the lower Susquehanna Valley, 15 to 40 percent of the water samples are above the drinking water standard for nitrate content. Soil testing enables farmers to gain optimum yields by applying only the nitrogen and phosphorous needed. Farmers who utilize the manure from their livestock may need to haul some of it to less endowed farmland.

This is especially true in Lancaster County, which has the highest dairy cow population per square mile in the United States. Here surplus nutrients have affected the drinking water of 175,000 people. One of the crucial bodies of water is the Conestoga River, a 60-mile tributary of the Susquehanna. The river handles some of the county's sewage as well as supplying drinking water for the swelling population in new homes in its vicinity. It has been invaluable for centuries—for travel to the Susquehannocks even before settlers built mills along its banks in the 1700s.

Sediment that has eroded from fields and construction sites is another of the damaging payloads that finds its way into the Conestoga. Also, phosphorous attaches itself to soil and then increases its potency when it reaches water. The murkiness prevents the underwater plants that hide fish from getting sunlight. And the phosphorous feeds blooms of deep green algae that float on the water surface and rob stream life of oxygen. Farmers with foresight plant a groundcover on their meadow creek banks and on fallow fields. A fenced creek also prevents cows from polluting it.

At Walnut Acres, Paul Keane established an earth-sustaining farm long before it was acceptable to do so. Since 1946, his organic farm in Snyder County has raised its soil's humus and mineral content without the use of any pesticides or fertilizers. Ladybugs and praying mantises keep damaging insects under control. Sawdust, dried chicken manure, cannery wastes, pea vines and corn cobs build the soil. During the two fallow years in a five-year crop cycle, green rye and alfalfa cover and nurture the soil. The raising and processing of grains, vegetables, fruits and organic-fed beef is a sustainable cycle. Besides feeding people well and enhancing the environment, Walnut Acres rings up multi-millions in annual sales. The whole endeavor rests on an attitude that was expressed by a Native American chief and is printed on the farm's packaging: "This we know: the earth does not belong to man; man belongs to the earth. All things are connected."

Encouraging the earth's production of their food gratifies a rural family. The rhythms of tending go on from early March when they watch the first asparagas tips poke out of frost-tinged mulch to the November day that they pick the last winter squash. Surplus vegetables, certainly some zucchini, are preserved, shared or sold.

The place to take the biggest tomato and the finest calf is the county fair held at the end of summer. Fairs began in colonial times to showcase agriculture and to unify the rural community. York holds the oldest in the state and possibly in the nation; it got its start in 1765. Even though big name entertainers in the grandstand have replaced fiddling and clogging contests, and stands sell food to the attenders who brought picnic baskets during the early years, the crux of the fair is the judging. Ah, the satisfaction of a blue ribbon!

In Adams County, orchards line the rolling hillsides that nestle against the ridges of South Mountain. The county ranks first in Pennsylvania's production of apples and turkeys and second for peaches and eggs. At its apple festival, the cider presses squeeze and the cauldron of apple butter boils while the music rolls.

Fruit farms and vineyards add to the beauty of York County, which even boasts of its own crunchy apple, the York Imperial. Orchards offer pick-your-own fruits, ready-to-bake pies and prime specimens shipped anywhere. An orchard drive during spring blossom time is scenic, and the small pink buds on grape vines multiply into a glorious, frothy show. The Lancaster and York grapes that hang lush and heavy five months later are crushed into award-winning fruity wines.

When the vine is bare and shrivelled, and the foxes cagey in their holes, the hunt is on. Yes, York County sports two recognized fox hunts. One, the Rose Tree Club Fox Hunt, is one of the oldest in the country. In the frosty November air, Mrs. Shoemaker's Weybright Hounds, the first pack to bear a woman's name, hear the rousing call of the huntsman's horn and pursue a scent across fields into a small stand of timber. Chasing the hounds cross-country, the horses gallop a solid four miles.

There are other reasons that Yorkers refer to their county as "horse heaven." Hanover Shoe Farms is the largest standardbred nursery in the world. Spring Valley Park is equipped for dressage and cross-country jumps. Horse lovers ride the ridge roads to enjoy vistas of tilled valleys and tree-topped thickets. Some take advantage of riding trails in the County's 8,000 acres of park land.

In the countryside, life dares to slow a bit. Folks on the Isle of Que at the edge of Selinsgrove relax on their hammocks and benches along the bank, facing the river. Along a rural route when the mail carrier's car peels away in the gravel, it is time to sit on the porch swing and read this week's paper. A picnic of homegrown foods finishes off a day of working in the fields. Evenings disappear quickly during a game of croquet or dominoes with the neighbors. With the coming of night, the stars rise poised and plentiful, filled with the promises of farming the land through the ages.

(PREVIOUS PAGE) Gourds, The Farmer's Daughter, a garden center, Shrewsbury, York Co. (UPPER LEFT) Farms and stream, northern York Co. (UPPER CENTER) Child blowing dandelion seeds, Northumberland Co. (UPPER RIGHT) Strawberries for sale from farm, Stritc's Orchards, Dauphin Co. (LOWER LEFT) Fruit pies for sale at orchard store, Maple Lawn Farms, York Co. (LOWER CENTER) Sheep shearing by Shirley, Terry and Scott (son) Womer at their farm, Middleburg, Snyder Co. (LOWER RIGHT) Apple blossoms, orchard, Adams Co. (NEXT PAGES) Aerial, agriculture in northern Dauphin County, facing southwest, with Halifax and Susquehanna River in distance.

(UPPER LEFT) Aerial,
ridges and narrow valleys,
Juniata Co., (UPPER
RIGHT) Powells Valley,
Halifax, Dauphin Co.
(LOWER LEFT) Grape
harvest, Nissley Vineyard,
Bainbridge, Lancaster Co.
(LOWER RIGHT) Hunts-
man Wm. Boggs Shoemaker,
MFH calling Weybright ·
Hounds in, fox hunt, Felton,
York Co.

(UPPER LEFT) Herb and Margaret Zeager and sons playing dominoes with neighbors Maurice and Rhoda Hartzler near Watsontown. (UPPER RIGHT) Farmland during winter, Dauphin Co. (BELOW) Breakfast after a November fox hunt, Weybright Farm, Felton, York Co.

10

The Lure of the Outdoors

A female hiker approached Jack's Mountain with an earnestness that sensed promise. Quaker naturalist Euell Gibbons must have shared this view because in the 60s he chose to live there in northern Snyder County to gather edible and healing plants for his well-known books on foraging. A cloud mist shut out the V shape of geese cackling overhead as the solitary walker plunged into full autumn foliage—the strong reds of gum trees, deep yellows of the beeches and birches and sugar maples, a blend of both.

A flicker pecked, and a covy of brown birds twittered in the underbrush. The path reached a grove dark with evergreens. Something rustled. For a long two minutes, the woman tried to track the source, facing one way, still. A maturing black bear had been sighted in the area recently. But not today. The movement must have been a squirrel residing in one of the leafy masses overhead. The hiker turned to continue up the grade. But she stopped, awash with a sense of having been watched. Twenty feet ahead, two young doe, bolted off the path. Their retreating white tails signaled their claim to the woodlands. The woman moved on with gratitude for the encounter.

Humans crave such experiences in the wild. Backpackers, campers, fishermen and hunters relish telling their "stories" of brushes with danger or of outwitting nature. Their enjoyment of the outdoors is dependent on the continuous protection of lands set aside for conservation and natural recreation. Once heavily lumbered, Jack's is one of numerous ridges within the Bald Eagle State Forest encompassing nearly 200,000 acres. Among its treasures are uncut tree stands at least 200 years old. Locals try to keep secret the "Tall Timbers" in Snyder-Middleswarth State Park. There giant hemlocks and white pines rise straight and tall a hundred feet from the floor of the narrow valley that cradles Swift Run. On nearby Paddy Mountain a natural amphitheater of virgin hemlocks supposedly inspired Joyce Kilmer to write the poem, "Trees."

Another 131 acres of virgin hemlock remain in the area of the Tuscarora State Forest that is near Big Springs State Park in Perry County. On a map, slices of slanted ridges lying northeast to southwest show areas of this 90,000-acre forest in Juniata and Cumberland Counties.

Our nation's first Forestry Bureau chief, Gifford Pinchot, left a legacy that becomes more valuable with the building of each new housing development. At the turn of the 20th century he pushed for planned saving of our forests, years before he became a governor of Pennsylvania in 1923. In northern York County, the state park named after him attracts thousands of campers and lovers of water sports. On a summer Saturday the 340-acre-lake at Pinchot may be the setting for a sailing clinic, for hundreds of swimmers, and for dozens of small craft from canoes to bass boats. A couple setting off in a bass boat called hopefully, "There are big ones in here, 23 or 24 inches!" A family in a 14-foot catamaran plied the lake to prepare for ocean sailing during their vacation. At dusk when a breeze brushed the pines, and cicadas buzzed in the woods, fishing boats turned on the required lights. Three young brothers continued to fish from the shore, standing against an almost-dark sky. "I got one!" whispered the shortest of the three, excitedly. It flapped and wiggled against the boy's grip. Their father appeared from a nearby campsite and verified that it was indeed big enough to keep.

Lake Marburg at Codorus State Park stretches its coves and points around 1,245 acres of water. From a picnic outlook off Marina Road, this water play area created by a dam built by P.H. Gladfelter Paper Company is an inviting scene. Windsurfers zip across the water; boats up to 24 feet and 10 horse power pull out of the marina. Canoes, kayaks and waterskiers slice the surface at varying speeds. The lake feeds a 680,000-gallon pool, famous for its island. Campers can select a site with a grassy playing field out its backdoor.

City families who can muster through packing and driving Friday night are rewarded with a wonderful wakeup by the birds or the raccoons Saturday morning.

Kayaking, tubing, sculling and powerboating go with the Susquehanna. The riffles at the Dauphin Narrows, marked in the 80s by a makeshift version of the Statue of Liberty, challenge kayakers. Some paddle south of the Rockville Bridge to spot the egrets and herons that are summer boarders on Wade Island. When the leaves have fallen, it is time to scan the skies for a bald or even a Golden eagle.

Every year hundreds of hikers traverse the Pennsylvania section of the Appalachian Trail which heads north from Adams and Cumberland counties into Perry, Dauphin and Lebanon. Its varied route borders fields over fence rows, glides through the towns of Duncannon and Boiling Springs, crosses the Susquehanna over the Clark's Ferry Bridge, ascends Cove and Peter's Mountains and plunges into 30,000 acres of Stony Mountain gamelands, the largest roadless section in southeastern Pennsylvania. The trail's regional headquarters are in Boiling Springs, the site of a lake fed by deep springs that spout more than 20 million gallons of 53-degree water every day. Nearby is LeTort, a trout stream prized world-wide by those skilled in fly fishing.

Feeder streams of the Susquehanna give many residents pleasurable outings. For relief on a steamy day, hikers pad along Tucquan "winding water" Creek, one of the state's designated Wild and Scenic Rivers. It flows through a deep ravine where members of its protectorate, the Lancaster County Conservancy, has identified 21 species of ferns and twice as many different species of spring wildflowers. Mature oaks, hickories, maples and hemlocks add to the wonder of this Nature Preserve. Twisting energetically, the stream spills over room-sized chunks of rock, known as Wissahicken schist, carving saucers and forming cooling pools before dropping with a rushing roar to the finish, the wide Susquehanna.

On a fall morning when a fox is likely to appear, or rather slip by, the pawpaws near Kelly's Run or Pequea Creek are bound to be ripe. This green fruit with custard-like flesh must have pleased the palate of the Susquehannocks.

Across the river, Otter Creek also breathes coolness into the faces of its visitors. The sound of laughter ripples from the deep falls pool and the sun-splashed rocks above. Old hemlocks and the large-petaled leaves of umbrella magnolia trees bring the Pennsylvania state tree into closeness with a distinctively Southern species. The mosses and rocks of this gorge hold remarkable beauty. The view of the river and the scenic Urey Islands from the rocky face of Pioneer's Leap is a reminder of other outdoor highs within its watershed.

Spring spreads a carpet of a million Virginia bluebells and just as many white trillium at Shenk's Wild Flower Preserve. This soil, rich in limestone, feeds 150 species of wildflowers each April. Months later, on new snow, cross-country skiiers glide over Hershey's golf courses, past Shoaf's Mill in Perry County, and across fields in Snyder County.

Natural change and human imprints have given and have taken possibilities for enjoyment and recreation. Floods, erosion, preservation, building, damming and planting have all played a part in shaping the land and water that people experience for sport and pleasure. In the Susquehanna watershed, folks find in nature and the wild what the human spirit needs, as Euell Gibbons did.

(PREVIOUS PAGE) Bald Eagle State Forest, Snyder Co. (UPPER LEFT) Biking, Fishing Creek Valley, Dauphin Co. (UPPER RIGHT) Wind-surfing, Codorus State Park, York Co. (LOWER LEFT) Kayaking, Susquehanna River at Dauphin Narrows. (LOWER RIGHT) Sweep rowing on Susquehanna River near Sunbury.

(PREVIOUS PAGES) Tucquan Glen, Lancaster Co. (UPPER LEFT) Fishing, Susquehanna River near Sunbury. (UPPER RIGHT) Picnicking, Buffalo Springs State Park, Perry Co. (LOWER LEFT) Cross-country skiing, Riverfront Park, Harrisburg, (LOWER CENTER) Muddy Creek, a favorite for tubing, York Co. (LOWER RIGHT) Otter Creek near campground, York Co.

(PREVIOUS PAGES)
Bicycle racing, in front of
Capitol, 3rd St., Harrisburg.
(UPPER LEFT) Downhill
skiing, Ski Roundtop, York
Co. (UPPER CENTER)
Fishing at Rockville Bridge.
(UPPER RIGHT) Fishing on
Susquehanna near Harris-
burg. (LOWER LEFT)
Sailing, Gifford Pinchot State
Park, York Co. (LOWER
RIGHT) Kayaking at
Dauphin Narrows, Dauphin
Co.

(UPPER LEFT) Young birch leaves, Dauphin Co. (UPPER CENTER) Hiking, Swift Run Trail, Snyder-Middleswarth State Park, Snyder Co. (UPPER RIGHT) Bird-watching near Appalachian Trail, Pine Grove Furnace State Park, Cumberland Co. (BELOW) Fly fishing on Yellow Breeches Creek, Cumberland Co.

Reading Sources

Barton, Michael, **Life By the Moving Road: An Illustrated History of Greater Harrisburg**, Windsor Publications, Inc., Woodland Hills, 1983.

Beers, Paul B., **Profiles from the Susquehanna Valley**, Stackpole Books, Harrisburg, 1973.

Beyer, George R., **Guide to the State Historical Markers of Pennsylvania**, 5th ed. Commonwealth of Pennsylvania, Harrisburg, 1991.

Bitner, Jack, **Mt Gretna: A Coleman Legacy**, Lebanon County Historical Society, Lebanon, 1990.

Blockson, Charles L., **The Underground Railroad in Pennsylvania**, Flame International, Inc., Jacksonville, NC, 1981.

Bonta, Marcia, **Appalachian Spring**, University of Pittsburgh Press, Pittsburgh, 1991.

Carmer, Carl, **The Susquehanna**, Rinehart & Co., Inc., New York, 1955.

Geyer, Alan R. and Wm. H. Bolles, **Outstanding Scenic Geologic Features of Pennsylvania Part 2**, PA Dept. of Environmental Resources, Harrisburg, 1987.

History of Cumberland and Adams Counties, Pennsylvania, Warner, Beers & Co., Chicago, 1886.

Horton, Tom, **Bay Country**, The John Hopkins University Press, Baltimore, 1987.

Klein, Frederick Shriver, **Lancaster County Since 1841**, Lancaster, 1955.

Kraybill, Donald B., **The Riddle of Amish Culture**, The Johns Hopkins University Press, Baltimore, 1989.

Lawrence, Bill, **The Early American Wilderness**, Paragon House, New York, 1991.

Palmer, Tim, **Rivers of Pennsylvania**, The Pennsylvania State University Press, University Park and London, 1980.

Pennsylvania Writers' Program, **Pennsylvania: A Guide to the Keystone State**, Oxford University Press, New York, 1940.

Singmaster, Elsie, **Pennsylvania's Susquehanna**, J. Horace McFarland Co., Harrisburg, 1950.

Steinmetz, Richard H., Sr. and Robert D. Hoffsommer, **This Was Harrisburg: A Photographic History**, Stackpole Books, Harrisburg, 1976.

Wood, Jerome H. Jr., **Crossroads: Lancaster, Pennsylvania 1730-1790**, Commonwealth of PA, Harrisburg, 1979.

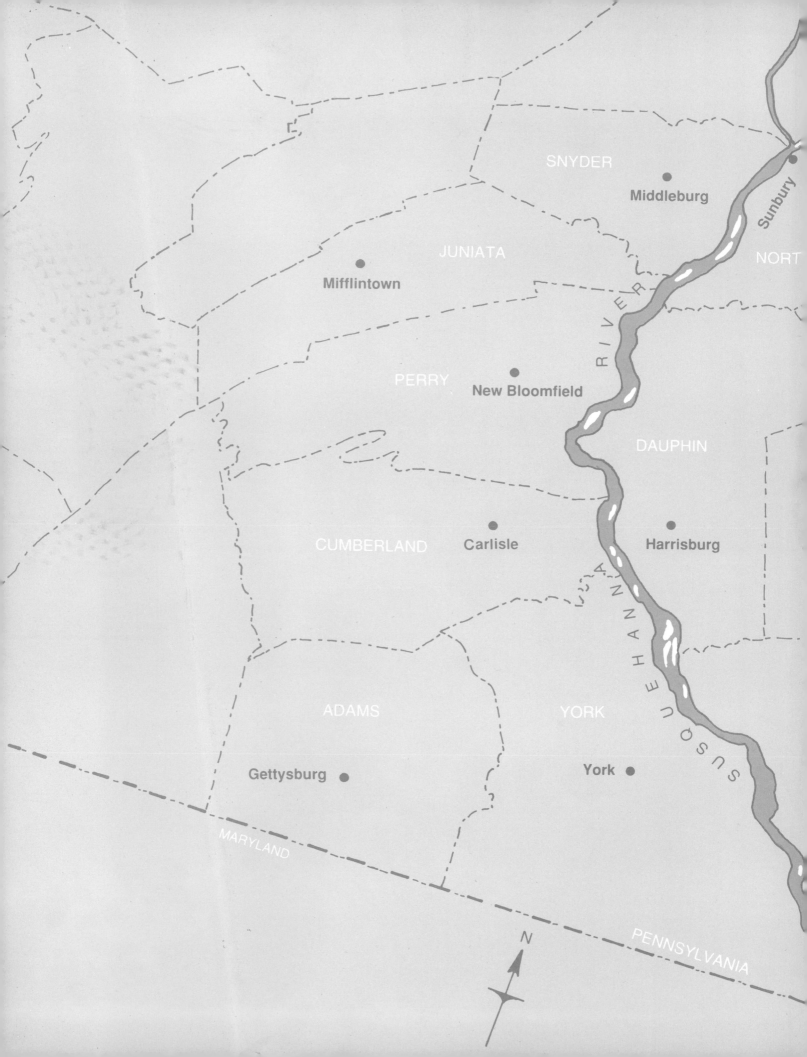